A Kid's
Best Friend

To my two 'best friends' Seeger and Murphy . . . woof—Alex

To Elena and Lidia and their best friend, Beijo—Maya

Editorial Offices: Glenview, Illinois • Parsippany, New Jersey • New York, New York
Sales Offices: Needham, Massachusetts • Duluth, Georgia • Glenview, Illinois • Coppell, Texas • Sacramento, California • Mesa, Arizona

A Kid's Best Friend by Maya Ajmera and Alex Fisher. Text copyright © 2002 Planet Dog Philanthropy and Shakti for Children. Photographs copyright © 2002 by individual copyright holders. Forward copyright © 2002 Planet Dog, Inc. Used with permission by Charlesbridge Publishing, Inc. All rights reserved.

Big Book version of *A Kid's Best Friend* published by Scott Foresman.

ISBN: 0-328-16877-7

Copyright © Pearson Education, Inc.

All Rights Reserved. Printed in the United States of America. This publication is protected by Copyright, and permission should be obtained from the publisher prior to any prohibited reproduction, storage in a retrieval system, or transmission in any form by any means, electronic, mechanical, photocopying, recording, or likewise. For information regarding permission(s), write to: Permissions Department, Scott Foresman, 1900 East Lake Avenue, Glenview, Illinois 60025.

2 3 4 5 6 7 8 9 10 V008 12 11 10 09 08 07 06 05

A Kid's Best Friend

Maya Ajmera and Alex Fisher

New Zealand

Bhutan

Russia

A kid's best friend

United States

Indonesia

Canada

Ireland

is a dog

with big
 floppy ears,

United States

United States

a wagging tail,

Canada

and a wet nose...

...with a big tongue and sloppy kisses

to lick and tickle your face clean.

United States

A dog is a best friend

Colombia

India

Canada

for playing,
and rolling, 15

United States

and

running

Nigeria

like the

wind.

A friend for

Poland

Argentina

getting

United States

messy and clean.

United States

A friend for

United States

Canada

cuddling and feeding

and caring

Bulgaria

Mexico

 *Canada*

 *United States*

for each other

on
cold
mornings
and

Peru

Ecuador

United States

Benin

hot afternoons.

And when the day is over, shut your eyes with your best friend, **be a pillow,** and snuggle into **deep sleep.**

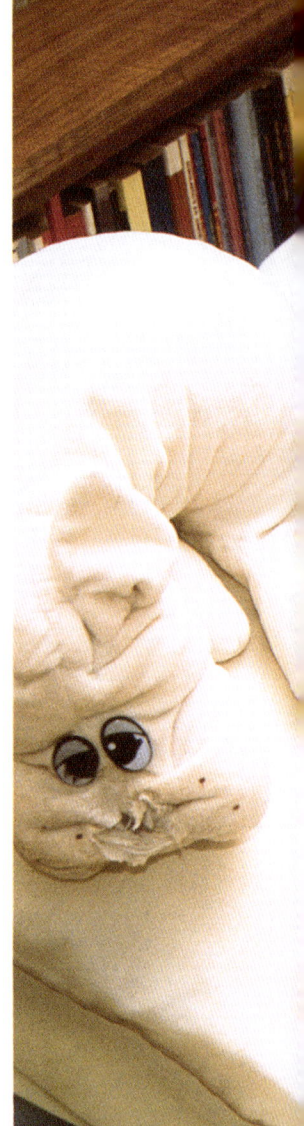

United States

France

A dog is a kid's

Australia

best friend.

All Kinds of Dogs

Just like people, no two dogs are the same. Some are big, while others are small, with long tails or short tails. Dogs can have stripes or spots. Their fur can be curly, shaggy, silky, spiky, long, or short. There are many different breeds, such as Chihuahua, a tiny dog originally from Mexico; Border Collie, from Australia; or Newfoundland, a huge dog from Canada. Many dogs are mutts: a combination of different breeds.

Having Fun

Dogs love to learn tricks. You can teach a dog to sit, play dead, roll over, shake hands, crawl, and even high-five. Dogs enjoy water. They jump and swim in rivers, ponds, and ocean waves. You may love to roll around in the grass or run around in your backyard with your dog. Like you, dogs love toys, especially squeaky ones that make noise. Dogs enjoy catching sticks and tennis balls. Dogs know how to have fun!

Special Care

Dogs are faithful friends, but they do need care. They have to be fed well and given water. Dogs love juicy bones and dog biscuits. Washing and scrubbing your dog is vital to its health. Their hair must be brushed and sometimes cut when it gets too long. Exercise is also important. Dogs can't go all day without exercise. You have to take your dog outside to walk and run and play.

Ways Dogs Serve

Dogs are important. They can protect you from harm by barking at strangers. They can serve as police dogs that help the police sniff out danger. Guide dogs help blind people live active lives. Because of their intelligence, strength, and keen sense of smell, some dogs are rescue dogs. Certain types of dogs help pull fishing nets or haul wood. All over the world, they help look after farm animals like sheep or goats. Dogs are an important part of your family and your community.

Your Best Friend

Your dog gives you unconditional love. In the morning, your dog jumps onto your bed to wake you. When you get home from school, your dog is waiting with a wagging tail, ready to make you happy. Like all best friends, dogs can sense your feelings. They know how to cheer you up when you are sick or sad by snuggling into bed with you or licking your face with loads of kisses. Your dog is your very best friend.

Special woofs to all the dogs at Planet Dog and Planet Dog Philanthropy for their generosity and support. To Maya, thanks for taking me on the journey and showing me the way, and to Jen for being there all along. Wag—Alex Fisher

My thanks to Alex for his creativity and friendship!—Maya Ajmera

Our heartfelt gratitude to Melany Kuhn for her superb design for A Kid's Best Friend. In addition, our thanks to Lindsey Heard-Maloney of Planet Dog Philanthropy and Stuart Maloney of Planet Dog for their enthusiastic support of this project. We would also like to thank our families.

Our thanks to all the photographers who participated in this project. Without the photographs, there would be no book. Many thanks to Peter Rapalus at Canine Companions for his support of this project.

A Kid's Best Friend is a project of Shakti for Children and Planet Dog Philanthropy.

Photographs: (left to right and top to bottom): Cover © 1997 Margaret Miller/Photo Researchers; Title Page: © Jeffrey Dunn, © Victor Englebert, © Nik Wheeler, © John Russell/Network Aspen, © Eastcott/Momatiuk/Woodfin Camp, © Victor Englebert; p.3: Arthus Bertrand/Jacana/Photo Researchers; p.4: © 2001 Jon Warren, © B & C Alexander/Photo Researchers; pp.4-5: © Victor Englebert; p.5: © Jeffrey Dunn; p.6: © Eastcott/Momatiuk/Woodfin Camp; p.7: © Porterfield/Chickering/Photo Researchers; p.8: © Nik Wheeler; pp.8-9: © Catherine Ursillo/Photo Researchers; p.9: © Eastcott/Momatiuk/Woodfin Camp; pp.10-11: © M. Schwarz/Image Works; p.12: © Victor Englebert, © Dinodia Picture Agency; p.13: © Carolyn A. McKeone/Photo Researchers; p.14; © John Russell/Network Aspen; p.15; © 2000 Jon Warren; p.16: © Eastcott/Momatiuk/Photo Researchers; pp.16-17: © Victor Englebert; p.17: © John Russell/Network Aspen; p.18: © Jeffrey Dunn; p.19: © Jeffrey Dunn, © Eastcott/Momatiuk/Woodfin Camp; p.20: © 2000 Jon Warren, © Dana Hyde/Photo Researchers; p.21: © Momatiuk/Eastcott/Woodfin Camp, © Canine Companions; p.24: © Victor Englebert, © Victor Englebert, © John Russell/Network Aspen; p.25: © Victor Englebert; pp.26-27: © Monkmeyer/Conklin; p.28: © Camille Tokerud/Photo Researchers; p.29: © Bill Bachman/Photo Researchers; p.30: © Porterfield/Chickering/Photo Researchers, © 2000 Jon Warren, © Eastcott/Momatiuk/Woodfin Camp; p.31: © Victor Englebert, © Jeffrey Dunn.